in soul alignment

AN ANTHOLOGY TO SUPPORT YOUR PURPOSE

BY SUSAN LOWENTHAL AXELROD

In Soul Alignment:
An Anthology to Support Your Purpose

ISBN: 979-8-218-28877-8

First Edition - September 2023

Published by JGU Press. Printed in the USA.

Design & Layout by Carasmatic Design - www.CarasmaticDesign.com

CONTENTS

PREFACE

What *is* alignment; what does it feel like and how do you get there?

These are questions I asked myself in my old Type A days when I needed to be in charge of so many things that all seemed a priority; and that way of being did not go well for me. By my late 30s I had an emotional meltdown that had me at home in bed for 10 days, no peripheral vision, feeling like I was in a fog and unable to cope. I ended up on anxiety and depression medication for 7 years.

I've shared my story in all four of my books, and still I repeat it here because I have learned that the evolution into a transformed way of being, the journey of enlightenment (AKA Soul journey to the light from the dark recesses of suppression) is supported by acknowledging how far you've come and takes consistent attending; reviewing and repeating your story and getting good at trial and error.

In my old Type A days of strived perfectionism, thinking I needed to be all things to all people and getting hijacked and triggered constantly from being unbalanced and ungrounded, I did not know the terms *resistance* and *alignment*. I had never even heard them. Early in my journey, as I sought out and began to learn from people who were already in enlightened or higher consciousness, I began to hear about alignment but still I could not relate. I could not connect with the word even though intellectually I knew the definition of it. I'm happy to say that today I can easily recognize it and I have tools to help me get there when I stray, connected back to my own self-energy, in soul alignment; this is what I call being in Soul Connection.

As I have gone deeper into my own awareness, I am now *conscious* of my thoughts, feelings, actions and of the hidden world that is in me. As such, I am more certain about how I want to be. No longer striving for perfection, I strive to be aligned with my Soul, in real time. Feeling deeply connected, and in charge of my thoughts, allowing my feelings to show themselves and be experienced. Yes, even in business! When I am truly aligned in the way I have described, my intuition deepens and business comes to me more easily. I feel much more in my purposeful impact space and my clients tell me their lives are changed from working with me. And, life seems easier with well-being achievable.

I invite you to join me on this journey of getting into alignment with your Soul. There may be some pitfalls along the way! We will breathe together through those and continue to rise in light.

INTRODUCTION

The Importance of Alignment

Dear Reader,

Why is being in alignment with your Soul important?

The answer is simple, it's transformative. When you are in Soul alignment you are more able to cope with and manage things that come at you. Especially the emotions that rise in response to, well everything really. And when you feel more in sync then you feel more on point and from there it's a fast rise to feeling a purposeful and meaning-filled life every day.

At least that's how it was for me. As my Younger Self, I was busy all the time and I felt like I could never get a handle on things; no way could I take time to meditate or even to 'breathe' as I was constantly being told. Thinking about taking time for myself was a farce. Later, in my maturing years, I realized that I was never taught the tools or given the permission to be other than the over-achiever I had become. And, certainly, in those days, I could never find self-permission. Later, in my maturing years, I began to glean why it was that I 'busied' myself. The choices I made were based on what I *thought* I had to do and the way I *thought* I had to be. I was in avoidance of feeling suppressed emotions. And, to be honest, I was in enmeshment with others.

I felt unsettled a lot. Today, I know the language for that–I was living in *resistance.* I felt unsure and unconfident as a young professional and mother. Oh don't get me wrong, I had high self-esteem and I knew that I was good at my job and 'doing well' in life. It's just that I kept asking myself, "Why am I so out of sorts?" And this: "What is my true purpose?"

The reason I speak, coach, and publish now is to share something I've learned: your purpose will show itself as you work to get more comfortable in your skin, to love and appreciate yourself more, to connect with your Soul, and allow intuition to rise. In the process, you will move away from the judgment you heap on yourself with toxic negative thoughts racing through your mind daily!

The reality is that you are born into a perfect state of soul-being. Every baby is perfect in her or his Soul, pure, unemotional, and unattached to self-judgment. But from our first day, forces conspire to create disconnection from Soul. Born into worry (all parents worry!), fear, anger, or even malevolent intention, the self-protective layers start to build up around us early, *often unknown to us,* and create emotional wounds that

You are born into a perfect state of soul-being.

can affect us for life. The layers create resistance that feels -at least- like being out of sorts, or -at most- being in utter personal emotional and spiritual disarray. My personal experience, and the basis of my work now, is that soul connection activity* helps us break through layers to get to the core of who we were meant to be, to know our true selves and live in confident well-being, purpose revealed.

Being in Soul alignment just feels better; feeling like yourself and comfortable in your skin. It's simply wonderful to be 'OK' with who you are, where you are in life, how you are, and all the rest. From there, that alignment helps you ascend into a lighter way of being. As you work towards this state, purpose will find you and intention will follow to meet up with the deepest soul desire, to be remembered. Soul confidence leads to legacy.

In this book, you will find among the chapters many different areas where we might find ourselves in resistance. My intention is for you to come to conscious awareness about what it feels like to be in resistance and to learn how to bring alignment into your life.

A word on vulnerability: One manuscript reader told me there are too many 'I's' in this book. 'I' laughed at that. If there's one thing I've learned on my crone lifepath to personal well-being, it's that showing imperfections and keeping it real requires someone to share vulnerabilities. I step into that for you so that you can learn from my experiences and develop your own practice, breaking through resistance, and being in alignment.

Wishing you the best always,

Susan

I have included in an appendix Chapter Six from my first book titled **Your Job Is To Be**, *an anthology to inspire soul-connection for you to learn about soul-connection activity. The chapter is called,* **Windows to Your Soul.**

1

IN ALIGNMENT WITH YOUR MIND

Thoughts are things. "What?" I asked myself as I listened to the first recorded book on my journey to self-liberation and enlightenment. I did not understand what was being shared. What did it mean? Aren't thoughts just, well, thoughts? How could a thought be a thing? But from a pain point in my own life transition from Type-A anxious living, I kept listening. During a two-year period of commuting to a somewhat distant work location, I turned my car into a university and I listened repeatedly to soothing voices helping me open to foreign ideas. The 'journey' included the physical experience of driving in solitude long enough distances for the material to begin to integrate into my brain (it was only later that the material touched my Soul).

Thoughts are things. Thoughts create feelings. Feelings create experiences. This progression was remote to me, even non-existent. As an achiever personality since my early teens, I had lived mostly in the 'doing' space and this supported me well through my high school years, and into my college and early adult decades. But during that time, I began to break down emotionally from always pushing to do more. As I reflect back, I do not know who I was trying to impress. No one else had higher expectations of me than me but somewhere from deep inside, I thought they did. I felt like I could never meet these expectations. Coming from a multi-generation high-achieving family, and doubtless from ancestral legacy, I felt my birthright was to succeed and to achieve. In order to accomplish this birthright, 'pushing' became part of my existence. Worrying and whining about nearly everything followed. Always outside of myself, I looked everywhere else to point and to blame.

In my car-university education, I opened to ideas that I had formerly derided such as self-love, being happy, the inner child, and higher consciousness. When I learned that thoughts were things and you can control things, my life lens grew clearer. I felt more in control of myself and my life. After an emotional meltdown in my 30s, through therapy, meds for a time, love and support from my family and friends, writing, exercise, and discovering nature, I found the basis of what I call enlightenment, my journey to the light. Now, I know it to be *soul-connection*.

I felt more in control of myself and my life.

And it all stemmed from taking responsibility for myself. That's what brought me 100% control. From a place of privilege, I had whined and blamed others. I hated myself for it. From education by other Seers and Masters and along the way on my journey, I learned to like myself, to feel deeply, and discover my soul. Eventually, I fell in love with her and that was the beginning of my rise as an adult, a crone, a Master, a Seer, and a Coach. Thoughts are things, you can control things. When you do, you will be in alignment with your mind and your soul will flourish.

self-reflections

2

IN ALIGNMENT WITH YOUR BODY

I look in the mirror and I love what I see. Oh, to be sure, it's not perfection. Or is it? I remember having cellulite on my thighs from my teens through my early mid-years and I hated them. I felt embarrassed in bathing suits and shorts. Even though I had a small waist and otherwise good proportions in the body I was born with, I held on to a nagging feeling about it for years that lay waiting inside me to show itself when summer arrived. I was not totally sedentary, and this was before the days of screens-in-hands or any kind of binge-watching, but the cellulite persisted. It became a lens through which I saw my whole-body image. And, in my mind, the lens was blurry and grey, not rosy and clear. How, then, I wonder, did that affect my mind and my soul? Where did a negative body image start for me when, by all accounts, mine was 'perfectly' fine?

I do remember my early years being somewhat active. We lived in an idyllic neighborhood where we walked to school, to a pond to skate, and to a neighborhood store, and I grew up skiing and going to a summer camp with all outdoor activities. In high school, I was a cheerleader for a few minutes, and I participated in a school-wide annual dance team show but was not 'into' sports and had no regular exercise practice. My inherent leadership characteristics showed early, and I participated in training and skill development activities. I spent the next four years organizing, leading, on the phone, sitting in meetings, and writing and speaking from a lectern. I went from there to a competitive women's college where road trips to co-ed schools were the most active thing I did until I nearly failed out and had to spend untold hours sitting in the 'libes' studying.

Moving from there into a traditional paradigm—married, work, house, dog, children, bigger house, more work, volunteering—and from there, into an emotional meltdown in my thirties. Then, and only then, did I start journaling in earnest (creativity), get myself into a dance class (with happy dance music), then into a gym (with rowdy workout music), and finally out into nature which led naturally into meditative space (where

I'm filled with gratitude for my physical well-being.

I started writing and publishing guided meditations). Inherent in this detailed journey are what I call the four 'windows to the soul'—music, creativity, nature, and prayer/meditation. Named thus, because, along the way, I met my own Soul. And she was lovely. Nearly perfect.

And a funny thing happened, I got into alignment with my body. So now, when I look in the mirror, I love what I see, and I'm filled with gratitude for my physical well-being. No longer interested in perfection, I commit to being in alignment with the physical body that serves my life, my purpose, my mission, and my legacy.

self-reflections

3

IN ALIGNMENT WITH YOUR SOUL

'But what if I could?' This question changed the trajectory of my life. After a breakdown from trying to be *"all that"* to everyone, my Soul finally buckled. One day, I just stopped. I had no choice. The tears came pouring out of me and immobilized me for days. I lay in bed, with no peripheral vision, inert, hardly able to form an active thought. That same week, my 5-year-old was home with strep throat, lying in a little made-up bed on the floor next to me. I lay in a fog saying to myself "How apt for my life right now. I'm having a breakdown and my child needs me and I feel like I have no support."

Was that true? All these years later, I must be honest, I don't know. But I could show you my journal entry that says I believed it, in that moment, in that time. Was there something, then, that I didn't see? Or, rather, was I seeing clearly for the first time?

Through medication, therapy, and an intentional journey that included healthier self-care and learning about mindset transformation, I got 'better.' Better enough to function again after only 10 days. That precious 5-year-old is now an adult. And I am in a confident and calm place that guides me, still, minute-by-minute on the journey of a lifetime. Today, off medication, with clear mind, and easy heart (mostly, still human though!), I feel, freely and without resistance. I'm self-connected (AKA soul-connected) much of the time with self-permission to expunge, explore, expound, and expand. This is soul alignment.

And, from my own journey to enlightenment, I coach other women in their second half to learn about, feel and get into their soul alignment through living a confident life. Open to intuition rising on this soul journey to Self-Love; permission given to grow and evolve into who you are intended to be.

We are all born with a divine gift but often intuition gets submerged in the 'doing' of life, and from the insecurities layered in from experiences of 'other.' Others who suppress our inner selves, intentionally or not; starting with our parents who sometimes love us so deeply they suffocate our independent Being. This is not criticism and not to be judged, just noted. Along your life path, it is up to you—100% in your control—to

We are all born with
a divine gift but
often intuition gets
submerged in the
'doing' of life.

be who you
want to be
and how you
want to be. To
connect with your
Soul (I define it as your
place of deepest feeling), break
free from the ties that bind, break out of the box you're
born into, and break through the resistance that keeps
you from being in self-sync. Commit, focus, and trust.
Being in alignment with your Soul, it's up to you.

self-reflections

IN ALIGNMENT WITH SELF-AGENCY

Life in your control. This concept can feel elusive when you allow thoughts to run roughshod. "What if this happens, what if this doesn't happen, what if it goes badly, what if she...what if he...I can't...she won't ..." Life in your control, how do you get there? Consider the phrase self-agency and you will begin to plot your own course to self-confidence, self-control, independence, and full sovereignty. This topic is not 'soft', it's vital enough that the National Center for Biotechnology Information (a division of the US National Institute of Health) offers a research paper on the topic in their National Library of Medicine. The article is called, *What Is the Sense of Agency and Why Does it Matter?* By James W. Moore (NCIB, August 29, 2016). The article Keywords tell the importance: consciousness, free will, responsibility, human-computer interaction, legal, aging, schizophrenia, OCD. In the article, Moore says that a sense of agency refers to *the feeling of control over actions and their consequences.*

In my work as a Confidence Coach for women, I find feelings of lack of agency to be constant. As an observer of the human condition and emotions now, it feels like the difficulties of living life through the Covid-19 pandemic pale in comparison to the epidemic of anxiety and depression. If you google 'anxiety and depression,' you get 859,000,000 results, a sought topic. The basis of anxiety and depression is a lack of self-control. I work with clients to discover and explore self-agency, a sense of being in control of self, life, and even destiny. One way to do this is to create a visual depiction for yourself of you in charge, in control, in the driver's seat. If you're a car enthusiast, find a picture of a car with a steering wheel that you're holding onto, keeping control, driving straight on, or turning right or left with a turn of your hands on the wheel. As you see this picture, invoke feelings of self-agency, you in control.

Another visual depiction that can serve your rise in self-agency is a picture of a horse, with you in the saddle, holding the reins. Horses are magnificent, majestic, and spiritual creatures. They symbolize freedom, confidence, and even triumph. When you're riding, you feel high up in the air, higher than your normal stance and when you're confidently in the saddle, you feel free and in charge. With the most subtle flick of one wrist, a horse will take your direction right,

You feel free and in charge.

left, or center; with a small pressure of your knees, a horse will speed up or slow down as you direct. Horses are intelligent and intuitive and offer healing just by being near them. They are broad and strong and instill a sense of calm confidence and peacefulness. In other words, you feel self-agency when you have the reins in your hand. Visualizing this will serve your alignment with self-agency; you, in control of your life.

self-reflections

5

IN ALIGNMENT WITH YOUR FEELINGS

How does it feel to be in alignment with your feelings? Do you even know? While worry, anxiousness, or depressiveness are familiar feelings for most people, feelings of contentment, satisfaction, and happiness seem elusive. I'm not sure if this is any different today than it has ever been in the history of the world, but this is our time. We are the stewards of humanity and the world, and it is up to us to be in alignment with our feelings to responsibly provide a happy and well future. It's hard to do this when you're feeling out of control.

If you are in a struggle and swirling in a negative place, sometimes it helps to figure out how to get to 'OK.' Excellent may be a better place to be, but just getting to OK moves you in the right direction. As a Coach, I help my clients get to 'OK' on the way to excellence. I use the visual of a platform-the Platform of OK-a solid place to stand where you can feel firm footing, even jump up and down confidently sure that the platform will hold you. When you are in any bad or negative place, sometimes it's hard just to get to OK.

Imagine a window washer's platform, that solid place to stand even high up in the air. When you're in a negative place, the platform is too high to reach; you can't even get your fingertips over the top to pull it down. Now imagine that the way to ratchet down the platform into your reach is by creating a simple positive thought. And each positive thought you think ratchets the platform down closer to you: "I want to feel better than this" [one ratchet down]. "I feel better when I am in control" [another notch]. "I decide how I want to feel; I want to feel OK" [another notch]. Then imagine getting your fingertips onto the edge of the Platform, firmly grasping it. Now use additional positive thoughts to bring it even closer: "I know what I want." "I take action to feel better" [another notch]. "I feel good now that I'm in charge" [another notch]. Then, imagine yourself pulling that platform all the way down to the floor in front of you, stepping up on it, and bouncing up and down a bit. How does it feel? Solid? That's what I call the Platform of OK.

Is this a mind game? It is. Will these mind games work for you? They might. Can this mind game hurt you? No. Why not give it a try? I learned the impact

I decide how I want to feel.

of mind games through my own transformative journey from resistance to alignment and now I teach them to clients. Thought reframing from the negative to the positive is a powerful tool if you commit to the outcomes you desire for your best life. Getting to the Platform of OK will help you on your way to being in alignment with your feelings and finding personal control.

self-reflections

6

IN ALIGNMENT WITH YOUR INTUITION

Alignment, a term that describes the wheels on your car or that feeling you have when your soul is seen? Before my own spiritual transformation decades ago, I thought of alignment as something that I needed to do for my tires every so often. Mechanics tell you that if your tires or suspension aren't aligned, there is uneven pressure on the tires that can cause your car to work harder on the tires than it needs to. This is my lived experience and an apt analogy for the way my life used to be, 'out of alignment,' and 'working harder than needed.' Stress leads to emotional distress which leads to the mental decline of anxiety and depression. And that landed me in bed for 10 days without any peripheral vision, crying uncontrolled and mostly inert. I learned what being out of alignment truly meant.

It took time for me to move to a new way of Being. I call it my journey to Enlightenment which included medication, love from my family, commitment to myself (learning what self-care and self-love meant), and a growing desire to want to feel better and to live differently. Eventually, my journey included exercise and finding Mother Nature who became my greatest cheerleader.

Now, I find this metaphor apt for being in Soul Alignment. It feels like you can take your hands off the wheel for a moment and know deep down that you will go straight forward in the direction you're headed; confident that you will not swerve one way or another. I've learned further that getting in alignment with your mind, body, and soul is best served by being in alignment with your intuition. Intuition is the gift anointed on you by the Divine upon your birth into this world. It's the feeling space of knowing. A woman's intuition-you have it and yours is yours alone. It is what makes you a Seer (every woman is) and understanding your intuition (explore it, you must) is a blessing. Intuition is one of the characteristics of divine feminine energy, a healing force desperately needed by humanity. A woman's intuition is yours if you see it. Do you? And more importantly, can you feel it? Being in

It's the feeling space of knowing.

alignment with your intuition is being in the deepest feeling space, a space of belief in self, soul, love, and confidence. A knowing space, with your suspension, aligned, working at your best, your most efficient; trusting yourself in deep soul-connection for the good you are intended to bring to our world. When you explore it and get aligned with your intuition, you can trust yourself, your choices, and feel well-adjusted. Passion and purpose bubble up, joy erupts and legacy ensues.

self-reflections

7

IN ALIGNMENT WITH ENTHUSIASM

When was the last time you felt enthusiasm rise in you? When was the last time you had the feeling of invigoration, adventure, anything outrageously awesome, or did anything that would be considered extreme? Are you an adventure goddess? Or, has it been so long that you can't even remember the feeling of adrenaline coursing through your veins? Of course, anxiety feels the same way and THAT may be familiar to you. But there's no fun in anxiety. Fun is important because it serves your playful soul and your playful soul serves to get you out of a fixed mindset (*Mindset* by Carol Dweck, 2015). In a fixed mindset, people believe their basic qualities, like their intelligence or talent, are simply fixed traits. They spend their time documenting their intelligence or talent instead of developing them. This can lead to a lack of imagination which after all is part of play. This is exactly what happened to me for many years. I would hear myself say, "I'm not good at imagination/play" and then I would be in amazement as I lacked 'play' in my life.

I learned about growth mindset from Dweck's book. "In a growth mindset, people believe that their most basic abilities can be developed through dedication and hard work—brains and talent are just the starting point. This view creates a love of learning and a resilience that is essential for great accomplishment."

I've grown the growth mindset muscle since I learned what it was called. To wit, last month, I drove cross country alone (twice), jumped out of a plane, walked cliffs overlooking the Atlantic Ocean, scaled a rock climbing wall, and ran in a bikini on a public beach. I also started a new business endeavor and committed to a new fit-life practice (Qigong). Such accomplishments!

What will it take for you to align with enthusiasm in your life? What will it take for you to give yourself full, unfettered permission to feel? In this case, feeling fun and frolic, freedom and festivity, joy and even abandon. All the things that you could feel easily when you were a child but began to be stripped away when you grew through childhood into young adulthood. Especially for women, responsibility came early as girls, taking care of our younger siblings, helping mommy or daddy, and more. Enthusiasm became subsumed to imposed

What would feel fun, invigorating, and outrageously awesome for me?

responsibility
and stripped
away our enlightened
openness in youth. But you
can bring it forth if you consider this question: What
would feel fun, invigorating, and outrageously awesome
for me? What can I do about it? What will stop me?
What will support me? Go there, do that. Get yourself
aligned with enthusiasm, your Soul and your future self
will thank you.

self-reflections

8

IN ALIGNMENT WITH NATURE

I can not think of something that has changed my life more profoundly than getting to know Mother Nature. Ironically, I got to know her in my effort to move through a depressive phase in my life. When I broke down emotionally from *too-muchness* in my thirties, 'trying' to do it all at the same time, I went on medication. I felt blessed to have good health insurance and a supportive husband and family and that helped me through the 'down' time. The medication eventually cleared away the fog. I learned that's how it works; it takes time and one day you wake up and realize you feel better, clearer, lighter, and even happier. I did it the best way—in conjunction with the medication I committed to talk therapy. I showed up, I met my feelings, and that was the start of my beleaguered soul raising her head and learning there was light 'up' there. Journaling helped immeasurably. Free writing also helped my soul's voice begin to be uncovered. I was on my way and I committed to that path simply because I wanted so much to feel better. As I felt better along the way, I stayed with it so I could continue to feel even better; a beneficial cycle in alignment with what God, the Universe, Spirit, and universal wisdom wants for us.

Seven years later when I was ready to get off medication, my doctor said this: "If you want to get off medication, go to the gym." And I did. When Spring came, I realized I could still get exercise by getting outdoors and it was beautiful! I started walking on our lovely street and actually seeing the natural beauty around me. Through my commitment to self-care, self-improvement, and self-love, I saw through eyes that were open in a new way. I acknowledged blue skies, warm sun, brown bark, green leaves, and colorful flowers. Then, I walked further down the main street to a nature preserve and I was hooked. I had previously taken our young daughters to the preserve and to outdoor parks, but my eyes were clouded by my to-do list. I was there (before cell phones) but my mind was constantly working on 'other' (life, work, relationships, volunteering), not able to be mindfully present. I didn't even know what that meant.

Mother Nature introduced me to mindfulness, to getting quiet, to the cycles of seasons (yes, I walked

I invite you to meet Mother Nature.

even in the snow and rain), and to renewal. For me, there was nothing like walking on the path, seeing all She had to offer, and learning to breathe again. The actual physical path I walked turned into my spiritual path of rebirth. This is all totally true. I believe I became reborn in a way walking the paths that Mother Nature set up for us ages ago. I invite you to meet Mother Nature. And when you do, say hello for me.

self-reflections

9

IN ALIGNMENT WITH YOUR ENERGY

What does energy feel like? I asked myself this question early on in my journey to enlightenment. That's what I call my journey to the light from the darkness of anxiety and depression. In the beginning, I just wanted to feel better than the malaise that had overtaken me. I was going about life, of course, but something was off course. Today, I can identify it as living in resistance, being out of alignment with soul energy. But in those days, I did not know what to do, how to feel, or how to get better. Over time, through therapy, listening to self-help books, long walks in nature, journaling, and a growing commitment to Self, I kept hearing about energy. Energy work, energy medicine, healing energy, energy in alignment, I had no idea what these things meant. And, I questioned, even mocked it all with ancestral disdain, and closemindedness stemming from fear of change.

When I hit my bottom, I asked myself: "But what if there is something to it?" What if I didn't block it, what if I simply allowed for the possibility that there could be 'something' to the ideas and concepts? That there could be something simple and powerful that could support me rather than being worried, anxious, depressed, fatigued, or depleted? What if learning about and using 'energy' could help me feel better and I'm blocking feeling better from an old belief system? After all, energy IS a real thing, as defined here: "The strength and vitality required for sustained physical or mental activity." And, "Power derived from the utilization of physical or chemical resources, especially to provide light and heat or to work machines." As I studied and processed both physical energy and consciousness energy, all of these words began to speak to me: 'strength,' 'vitality,' 'sustained,' 'resources,' 'light,' 'heat,' and 'work.' I thought about the various definitions of each of the words and began to transform my ideas to accepting there could be something outside of the former concrete thinking that had not served me well.

As I began to glean things about being aligned with my own energy, I realized that I had already experienced it. I knew it when I was experiencing my own kinetic energy. In those times, I was moving

Get quiet, grow still, and sense things keenly.

forward in
untold ways
at what seemed
like light speed. And,
when I felt stuck I was in stasis,
unmoving. As I came into more confident sync with
my mind and my feelings, I gave myself permission
to allow intuition to rise. And things began to flow in
the way of a current, just like energy. I could easily
get quiet, grow still, and sense things keenly in a way
I never had, using all of my senses in real time. And I
believed more. Being in alignment with your energy is
a gift of stillness, of self-belief, of intuition rising, and
of soul consciousness.

self-reflections

IN ALIGNMENT
WITH POSITIVITY

"You don't have to be 'good' all the time, you know." This is what a friend used to tell me when I talked about getting-to-happy or even just getting-to-good. In response, I used to say, "I know. That's not what I'm talking about. I'm talking about getting to OK, good is often too much of a stretch for many people." Now, I call foul on this. I do insist on good! Through challenges, emotional distress, hardship, and even trauma, it has been studied and researched and proven that being in Positivity can change the trajectory of your life. It did mine.

The book, *Positivity, Discover the Upward Spiral that Will Change Your Life* by Barbara Frederickson, Ph.D. was a game-changer for me. Because it's filled with scientific studies and analysis, it spoke to the masculine side of my brain needing 'proof' that positivity could be an actual tool for life success and a feeder to being successful in work, business, and career. For me, the place to start was my brain, asking questions and curiously imagining the possibility that things could be a different way than I had experienced them. Through my own reading, writing, speaking, and observing, I experienced life shifts that were surprising to me. When I thought positive thoughts, when I acted in a genuinely happy and positive way, the spirits of people around me rose and I began attracting upbeat positive, and happy people into my life and network. I practiced it repeatedly with the same exact outcomes. The key was that I used many tools so that it wasn't 'fake it 'til you make it' but rather committing to creating intentional good thoughts, feeling better myself, and sharing my 'good' energy with those around me. Through therapy, journaling, walking in nature, creating mindful meditative space, and reading/listening/watching things that were uplifting, I connected to my own good self-energy; my Soul rose.

The result was that I began to feel more comfortable in my own skin, I was able to engage in a healthy way with others, and I began to know what happiness, joy, and calm felt like. This may sound extreme as you read this, but my Type-A lifestyle choices had taken a toll on my mind, body, spirit, and relationships. And now, too, as a certified Trauma Informed Professional Coach,

Positivity could be an actual tool for life success.

I am more aware than ever that every human experiences childhood difficulties that could be considered traumatic and have lasting impacts if not cleared mentally, emotionally and consciously. I was no exception. I went on an intentional journey to positivity using tools learned from many authors, helpers, teachers, healers, and soul guides. Then, I read *Why Good Things Happen To Good People, How to Live a Longer, Healthier, Happier Life by the Simple Act of Giving* by Stephen Post, Ph.D. and I found more scientific evidence of the experience I was living. I found myself in alignment with positivity, giving more, doing 'good,' and finding a deep and meaningful confident existence along the way.

self-reflections

11

IN ALIGNMENT WITH LOVE

What happens to girls as they turn into women? Little girls are the happiest, most outgoing self-loving creatures. "Mommy, I'm beautiful, aren't I!" It's an exclamation, not a question. Declaring to self and to anyone who listens, "I love myself!" At ages 4, 5, 6, 7, and 8 she is swirling and twirling, climbing up onto the bathroom vanity to look adoringly at herself in the mirror in total self-love alignment. Then, along the way of ages 9, 10, 11, and 12 things begin to shift. By middle school, self-loathing is commonplace, shoulders slump, insecurities are voiced, emotion is suppressed, and enthusiasm is dimmed. Self-love is gone and it takes years to get back. For some, it never returns.

What if you looked for it, though? What if you think

about it, make a conscious decision (that, itself, requires a breakthrough), and commit to loving yourself again? Why is this important? Because to be in alignment with soul; to design and live the life you want, you need to be in alignment with love. Love is one of the greatest powers on the planet. We see this in any momma-bear energy (whether she has two or four legs). The love of another for her offspring, in fact, the love of a woman–mother or not–has changed the course of history many times over, no? Why do we stay in utter resistance to it for ourselves? Why do we have to love everyone else and treat ourselves in the shabbiest unacceptable ways, mentally, emotionally, and physically?

What would it feel like to love yourself again? It took me years to learn. I had no idea that I had stopped loving myself until I had my emotional breakdown and went into therapy and started on a spiritual journey to break through the layers that had built up over 20 years of living a woman's life, even a good one. When you've lived in difficulty or trauma it's all the harder to connect to yourself in a loving way because you're mostly just 'trying' to survive. Right now, with these words, you have an opportunity to consciously seek out the love I'm addressing. Do you have it for yourself? If not, seek it out. Explore, discover, go after it, demand it of yourself. Do not yield an iota to anything other than feeling comfortable in your own skin, how you look is not the important thing here. Ask yourself how you feel about

Commit to loving yourself again.

yourself, about your life, about your future, and even about the world that you will be living in for the next few decades. All of this has to do with what love feels like.

Feel it for yourself, about yourself. It has been two decades since Louse Hay helped us learn about the importance of loving ourselves; looking in the mirror and saying "I love you." It sounded ridiculous to me until I had my breakdown. It became part of my breakthrough. If you haven't started yet, now is the time.

self-reflections

12

IN ALIGNMENT WITH SILENCE

For many years, I lived by the motto, "There's comfort in chaos." It was a placard I hand designed that lived on my college dorm door. In my early years, I developed into a Type A personality, moving and speaking quickly, busy all the time with activities of interest, engaged socially, attending programs and eventually leading them. I was content but I don't know that I was happy. I remember I used to say, "Happiness is overrated." Or, "being happy is overrated." In my early middle-years, mindfulness began to come into the mainstream from the alternative space created around it by the Industrial Revolution. Quiet, cared for main streets turned into frenzied selfish Wall Street with personal values submerged in the resulting noise.

Despite millennia of the silence of nature soothing

the soul, later centuries suppressed the same; silence got a bad rap for the mainstream. Mocked and marginalized as woo-woo, hippie and alternative, we allowed the men of Madison Avenue to make decisions for us and beyond that, the internet started embedding in our consciousness disrupting previous norms of quiet time or rest for the body, mind or soul. In today's collective consciousness, thumbs are frantically going, furiously responding to others in real time or participating in the new digital dopamine addiction.

But what happened to silence? Is it gone, subsumed in the resistance created from FOMO? No, it's not. The beauty of quiet can be yours whenever you want. If you get into alignment with how quiet serves, rest, walking, writing, even quiet talking or quiet playing can serve to soothe the soul. And from quiet, as your nervous system settles, as your brain synapses slow, you can find the beauty of silence. Silence. Silence in your heart and mind can be found whenever there is inner peace. And if you can't create it yourself, seek silence in nature, away from city streets, from crowds, from the constant disruption of perseverating negative thoughts, from the internet and all the resulting mania. Breaking through the resistance of conformity, seeking out the quiet and finding silence can support personal growth and a healthy evolution into the second half of life. It can break down negative thoughts leading to mental demise or even addiction. A healthier way

The beauty of quiet can be yours.

to live quietly serves the brain by relieving tension and stimulating new cell growth. Improving memory, mood and mindfulness, coming into alignment with silence can be a tool to extend life and love in relationships.

What can you do to find quiet in your life? Whether it's physical, mental, or emotional quiet, actively seeking it out, intentionally inviting it in will support you to be in improved personal alignment, in sync with a new life design. The beauty of silence does not compete with the beauty of a healthy active and engaged lifestyle, quite the contrary, it supports it in a way that serves a balanced wellbeing.

self-reflections

IN ALIGNMENT WITH GRIEF

In alignment with grief? Is that possible? I have learned that it is, but it does take understanding how grief and soul can work together.

Loss of all kinds can stop you dead in your tracks. Whether it is a long sustained loss from illness or a sudden loss from things completely out of your control, you can lose all sense of ground. I'm not sure there is a human alive who hasn't experienced some kind of loss that becomes grief, whether or not death has been a cause. The good news is that as we move slowly into a new world of higher consciousness, grief is allowed to be acknowledged. Earlier generations had to stick it out, keep it in, fight to breathe, and it felt as if no one cared because no one addressed it with you or for you. To be sure, this is all still a work in progress in the evolution of humanity.

I have learned through my own personal loss and grief journey that there is something we can do to be more aligned with grief. We can tend to our own hearts and souls. We can weep and wail inwardly to acknowledge the feelings and begin to process them for ourselves. We can create quiet space and allow stillness to visit and feel what there is to feel to allow emotions to work through rather than getting suppressed and stuck inside, possibly leading to mental unwellness or a health disorder. It may take a self-care focus that might be unusual for you and therefore not comfortable at first but persist!. These mindfulness opportunities are called practices for a reason.

On my own Soul Journey, as I rose in lightness of being from getting in control of my own thoughts and mindset, it became easier to see that the only permission I needed to receive was my own. Oh, but this wasn't easy. Not well modeled by the women before us, and surely not by the men. 'Wearing your heart on your sleeve' meant that you were overly emotional, not strong and stoic and worthy of leading. Men were mocked, women decried as having 'hysteria.' Grief was denied, feelings were soft, actions were lauded. Possibly, or even probably necessary for the times.

As I began to be more brave about showing my vulnerabilities by naming my grief and sharing its impact, there was deep resonance from others, a near

You help grow
a deeper world
consciousness.

universal
permission
fully granted, to
be as I was. Along the
way, after sitting in, processing and
integrating my grief, I began to imagine with evolving
clarity, being on the other side of a grief episode,
curiously looking for lessons and sharing the lessons
learned with others. Through a lens of love, I developed
a deep desire to grow and a keen vision to transform
through my experiences. Coming into alignment with
grief, being clear about what's affecting you and getting
brave to claim that space, outwardly showing your
vulnerability, helps to process feelings and integrate
emotions. In so doing, you help grow a deeper world
consciousness, helping others to understand, they
are not alone in their grief, creating connectedness
in humanity that is an antidote from the isolation of
stuffing feelings deep down inside you, under your
surface.

self-reflections

14

IN ALIGNMENT WITH HAPPINESS

It seems like it should be easy to be happy, all rainbows and flowers and chocolates. But then, rainbows come after a rain, flowers come with weeds and chocolate comes with fat, no? In my depressive days, that was the lens I saw through all the time. I could see and experience the good but there was always resistance to the full feeling, I think. It's hard to look back and to be sure, but I do have my journals that go back decades and I know this was a common outlook throughout. I do not know why, I was lucky and blessed to live a pretty normal life, ah, but yes, there were secrets to keep. Every child has secrets to keep, from the whispers of the night to sights seen from imaginations running wild. The child-mind is immature and untamed and resulting thoughts eventually embed as fears under the surface.

For many, the fears subside into the recesses of the mind, but as you grow older, weeds form, becoming an entangled mass of thoughts and feelings that clog your mind. These thoughts, now deeply rooted in your cells, can turn into disease, even if only a diseased mind of negativity, shame, self-loathing, guilt, judgment, or other detrimental issues. Does this sound harsh or unlikely? Think again. Most of us live with difficult feelings under our surface that steal the moments of joy or happiness that we seek and need. Then, we might gravitate towards activities that allow us 'not to think,' but what that really means, is not to *feel*.

And then, what of happiness? How can you come by it when you are burdened, sad or staying in the difficult past or concerning future? Be honest with yourself, do you know what happy feels like for you? In my coaching sessions, I have asked clients this question countless times. The common response is first, "I have to think about that." Followed later by, "I just don't know the last time I felt really happy." Most of us yearn for it, engaging in dopamine-hit activities to get that feel-good moment that we think is 'happy.' But is it? Take some time to consider this. Is happiness now the same as happiness in your Younger Self? If so, what are the activities you can bring forward into your adult life for this experience? Or, what is your maturing outlook of happiness now? Is happiness a thing to do or a thing to feel? What would being in alignment with happiness be like?

Do you know what happy feels like for you?

Soul-connecting activities can support your exploration. Do anything creative, listen to uplifting music, go out anywhere in nature, find the quiet within and connect to your Universal Source through prayer, meditation or mindfulness, engage in physical activity to get your heart pumping and systems in go-mode, or engage with animals any way you can. Soul-connection helps you become consciously aware of what it means to be present, in the here and now, feeling invigorated and alive. Happy moments of conscious awareness that allow you to do more, give more and impact more. Finally, hang with like-minded people, committed to living lives of full expression in alignment. Happiness is waiting for you!

self-reflections

IN ALIGNMENT
WITH NORMAL

As a child growing up, normal is the life you live. Until the time that contrast shows itself to you, you simply swim along the surface directly ahead as you were shown and as you were taught to do. The rights, rituals and requirements of life as you know it become rote, creating familiar patterns that become the habits of our lives. This is normal to you. Whether a nightly bedtime story or nightly beating, your child-mind holds on to your experience as an existence that 'everyone' lives. For most, these experiences will embed deeply under the surface and will show up throughout life as messages to the brain of what is 'supposed to' be, for you. And subconsciously, you hold onto the thought, 'this is what life is,' and you impose this 'supposed to' on the people who come into your life, either peripherally–

and they are not generally impacted, or integrally–and their normal likely does not mesh with your normal. Conflict can ensue. Sound familiar?

As you grow and are exposed to other people, other ways to be, other philosophies, and religions, expressions–in other words, other norms–then you might begin to question things for your Self (in connection with others) and for others (in connection with you). Coming into this conscious awareness is not an easy journey. It takes commitment to personal wellness, which can feel discordant if it has not been taught to you or modeled for you. Challenging your Self with questions that stir the Soul is one way to break through mindless malaise and ascend to mindful meaning exploring your personal values as separate from those of your upbringing. Am I doing what I want to be doing? Am I being the person I want to be? Am I showing up, sensing and sharing? Am I thinking thoughts of my own making, am I feeling?

When the Soul is stirred, you feel. And this may be way out of your norm, feeling feelings was possibly suppressed-at best-in your home of origin, or beaten out of you-at worst-literally or figuratively because feelings are the deepest expression of Self and everything is easier when Self is subjugated. No Voice, no autonomy, no conflict. This might lead to a feeling of being in resistance with Normal, a You you don't like.

What if you make a decision to design your life in consciousness?

It is possible you may be in awareness of this and you might want to change it as you go forward in mature relationships but you simply don't know how, because it's your normal.

But what if you came to awareness about all of this, and seek and find some clarity around the norms of your upbringing and the purposeful direction you want to move in, in your maturity? What if you make a decision to design your life in consciousness, creating a Normal that better matches the You of now? You can start this intentional process of coming into Alignment with your new Normal by getting quiet, exploring your depths, considering your experiences and especially by seeking out feelings and allowing rather than suppressing emotion. When you define your new Normal for You, getting in sync with it offers peace of mind and heart...embrace it, and enjoy.

self-reflections

16

IN ALIGNMENT WITH LIFE, SELF ACCEPTANCE

hat is it about life? Why is it so hard? Really, why? Every thought perseverates, every feeling weighs heavy. As a young child, thoughts mean nothing. You think, act, speak, and move on. You don't hold on to 'meaning' or feelings connected to thoughts until you're taught to do so. Then, imbued with legacy, societal or family impositions, thoughts get attached to feelings and you're off to the races. For the middle years of life, wheels in motion, you do the things you were taught, the things you were told and the things that you think will make you happy because, well, you're just 'supposed to' do it this way. This may look like the exact way of your family because that's all you know, or you may do things the exact opposite of the way of your family which you could see didn't work out well for them. Often racing ahead at lightspeed to get to the 'there' of imposed expectation, or perhaps to get to the Hallmark life you came to believe could be true for you. Some race ahead to achieve, some to avoid. Avoid what? Secrets. You might think you are the only one but most humans have them.

From the time your brain comes into cognition, you begin to see and hear things, such as yelling or whispering. From there, you begin to glean things and this is where your secrets start. Through an immature filter, the 'Don't tell' you hear from others leads to 'Don't say anything' – that is you telling your young Self a message from your observation-turned-experience; anger or anxiety, silence or shunning, predation or placating, fabrication or farce. Your young mind not understanding the why but your heart realizing the *what*, the not-good feelings which begin to affect your Soul. Your precious Soul, the place of deepest feeling, sinks down into the dark recesses over time as you begin to dress in the 'I should' or 'If only' shroud that informs your growth.

All of this, then, leads to non-acceptance of Self, in loathing or in fear. You do the best you can but deep down, you just feel not certain, perhaps not secure. And resistance settles in, deep in your being. Stealthy, insidious, it seeps into the crevices of your

What does self-acceptance feel like?

brain resulting in becoming inured to the deprecation of Self.

But, Alignment! What of it? What is it? What does it feel like to be in alignment with life? An important question-how can you know if you don't know? What does self-acceptance feel like? Again, how can you know if don't know the feeling of loving your Self?

Not taught in school, not truly promoted at home, certainly not learned in business! This, then, is your opportunity. Ask yourself, often, "Am I enough?" "Am I good enough?" Right here, right now, is this enough for now? Not that you won't forge ahead, dodging and dipping, swaying and sinking; surely you will, human that you are. But can you find a moment-perhaps this very moment-with full self-permission to just Be, to Be in alignment with Self, with your life as it is now-not as you yearn for it to be? What if 'here' was enough for now? What if life as you created it to now was perfect?

What if you felt happy, calm and peaceful with who you are and how you are, now? AKA, in alignment with your life as it is. In acceptance of Self-this is what I mean by being connected to Self-energy, or being in Soul Connection.

Someday, your end will arrive. I've learned that you don't know when that will be. All the material things will be gone, but the spiritual consciousness of alignment serves to the very end, and perhaps beyond. Why wait for the freed Soul consciousness of death? In Alignment with life, in Self-acceptance, how about freeing your Soul here and now?

self-reflections

In Soul Alignment, Where to From Here?

Dear Friend,

When we started our journey together at the beginning of this book, you were a 'Reader,' but now, after baring my soul to you through the chapters, and you sharing your soul through your journaling, you are my 'Friend.'

How did you do with the thesis of coming to and being in Alignment? Do you get it a bit more now? This idea, this concept, this way of being will be good for you! It will help you feel confidently comfortable in your skin. In the end, this is what most of us want. And, do you know, it's not too much to ask.

But "How?" you may ask! As with all good things, practice is the order of the day. The masters and monks know it. Daily practice leads to familiarity, familiarity leads to confidence, and confidence leads to discipline. Discipline leads to new created pathways that support your life. This process can also lead you away from old patterns of behavior born of resistance. Here's a Daily Alignment Practice for you to use, truly simple, quick, and effective:

Stand up comfortably or lie down quietly. Wriggle your body a bit to make sure everything is loose, not tense. Rub your hands together to create friction then hold them just an inch apart from each other for a moment. Then, take both hands and place one on top of the other over your heart. Take a long, slow, deep breath in and out of your nose. Now, take your hands and place one on top of the other over your abdomen and take a long slow, deep, breath again. Stay there a moment, quiet, centered, and comfortable. Take another long, slow, deep breath and just Be. Comfortable in your skin, mind quiet, soul at rest. When you do your breaths, do them with intention and fully extend on the slow exhale, blow all the air out from your chest and belly that you can (gamechanger).

This is what alignment can feel like. You can get there with this brief, and simple exercise. It works best if you start with an intentional thought, "I am comfortable in my skin, I am in alignment." Or, you can create any intentional thought you want, including "I am safe." I say this because I've learned through my work that many women need to affirm safety, if not from the physical, then from mental, emotional or even spiritual unsafety that gloms onto us from a young age. It may be in there, nagging at your Soul creating resistance. This book on Alignment is intended for you to get connected to the good Soul, the pure Soul, the Soul of your best existence so that you're in charge and in control which is what leads to confident purposefulness. I call this Soul Confidence. And if there's one thing I know, it's that Soul Confidence leads to Legacy; inarguably, a human's greatest wish, to be remembered after they're gone, to have made some kind of difference in the world. Coming into self-alignment gets us connected to our center, the place of Knowing. And Knowing supports your creation, designing your life in the way you want it to be, feeling on-point, in purposefulness, clear and certain, here and now.

Wishing you the best on your Soul journey in alignment. Please stay in touch.

With love,

Susan

IN SOUL ALIGNMENT

Questions to Consider

I speak about Soul-Connection to others all the time, people thank me for having these deep conversations. You can bring deeper soul meaning into your life by having Soul conversations with others, too. Here are a few questions to get you started:

- Do you know what being in alignment feels like for you?
- Where are you on your journey to living in an aligned state of being?
- What prevents you from feeling good/comfortable inside, AKA, aligned?

- Can you identify what being in resistance feels like for you? What does it feel like?
- What are some areas of your life that you live in resistance?
- What keeps you in resistance, AKA in inner discord?

- Which alignment in this book can you most relate to?
- Have you achieved it?
- If so, how did you come to that alignment?

- Where do you feel most aligned in your life?
- Where do you need help with alignment in your life?
- With whom can you speak about this honestly, in truth?

- What alignment or techniques would you suggest to others?
- What daily practice of alignment has worked for you (assuming you've integrated one into your life!)

- If you were telling your friend about alignment, what would you share?

Windows To Your Soul*

Is your Soul suffering? Are you aware of it? If you feel unclear, or that you lack focus or direction, it's likely that you are feeling soul-disconnect.

In the first decade, we're Super Girl, hands on hips with an 'I CAN' attitude. In the second decade, something happens. A shroud of mystery around blossoming womanhood, societal expectations, hormonal infusion and for many, a slow march to an externalized proclivity. How do I look, what does s/he think of me, why am I different from others, and the sway of the multi-hundred billion beauty industry assails our every sense. In the third decade, the 'I have to' starts. Whether growing a family or a career,

*This is Chapter Six from my first book, Your Job is To Be, referred to in the Introduction

whether partnered or alone, there's deeply internalized pressure to get it right, get it done, do it now. I have to...I have to...I have to.

Along the way, we become disconnected from our Soul, the strong, self-loving, spiritually-filled girl-child in us whose bright eyes see clearly, with purpose and love. By the fourth decade, you start yearning for 'more than this.' As a coach, often I hear 'I know I'm so lucky, but I feel empty inside.' Also, me...before I started my trek to a conscious existence that took my entire fourth decade. Then, I suffered for the onset of my 50th year, and now five years later, I feel free and connected.

I've learned and now teach others the tools which help you see; Windows to the Soul.

Prayer is the most obvious soul-connection; but if you pray, do you actually feel the linking with your Soul, with G-d? My own prayer-practice started with just attempting to clear my mind [heroic effort!], then moving to conquer a meditative space, then breaking through a fear-barrier of the greatest unknown [Is there a G-d?] to find prayer. Honestly, I don't 'get there' every time, but I know what it feels like now so I know where I'm heading.

Creativity is a multi-faceted gem offering your own formation, through your own senses and life experience to feel, find and connect. There are countless creative outlets you can use. You do not have to be 'an Artist' to construct the most fabulous creation of simple beauty to help you ascend.

Nature beguiles; its beauty and power can wrap you in an awe that can astonish the mind and spirit. From the simple acorn turned oak, to the colossal pounding of never-ending surf; from a cool breeze on a hot face to the phenomenon of a green leaf turning red, nature offers limitless opportunity to connect to your own Soul.

Song soothes and song stimulates. Have you felt it? Whether attending your first rock concert as a teen with the pounding base and exhilarating music making your heart rush or from a heartrending melody bringing tears to your eyes from its mournful rhythm… music can heal and help you connect more deeply than you can imagine.

To gain clarity in your life, choose any or all windows, clean them, open your eyes and look through to see your Soul, swaying, dancing, creating in joy on the other side.

WITH SUCH GRATITUDE

I would like to recognize my parents Therese Deborah Albach Lowenthal and Asher Arthur Lowenthal. I'm grateful to my core for the foundation they gave me, the love and support in all the early years of my life. I'm grateful for good genes in my family lineage and truly grateful for the commitment to and gift of the best education available. From formal classrooms in elementary through baccalaureate, to our dining room table to the Temple sanctuary; from summer camp bunks to the halls of Exeter Academy and all of the opportunities in between. I'm aware that I was born into blessing and while love was not overly articulated, it was ever-present in its way. In the end of each of my parent's lives, I saw their minds open up to accept a new way for me to be, full support, no offense taken to my choices to do things differently. I aspire to live this way for the rest of my days.

And to my mother-in-law Muriel Goldenberg Axelrod, a mother to me for 30 years, as sure as my own. She loved me unconditionally in full support of the woman I was becoming and the work I was creating. She was the first of my three parents to die, I was the only person in the room with her and I held my hands on my own heart but just could not bring myself to touch her body at the end. But as with so many things in my life, I learned from my mother-in-law so that when it was my father's time and then my mother's, I could be there, with my hand on their hearts as each of them took their last breath.

Though a grown woman myself now, a mother to my beloved adult daughters, Rebecca and Sarah, and to beloved adult nieces and nephews, I miss all three of these parents every day. Their love, wisdom and guidance supported me late into my years. I never took for granted how long they lived in my life. I pray for humility and unconditional love and acceptance of each of my own adult daughters so that they can live lives full-on, as I have done with the blessing of all three parents. Somehow, along the way of my maturity my parents stopped worrying about me and started trusting me and I intend to do the same for my own daughters. To Mom and to Dad, and to Mum, I feel you with me sometimes when I most need your wisdom, thank you.

One more thing. I was blessed to live long into my adulthood with 3 parents, but there are many young people who have lost parents at a young age. They need wisdom and guidance from other moms and dads in the world. I invite you, reader, to step up when you can. I aspire to offer that guidance whenever sought, to be that Momma when needed.

TESTIMONIALS

What I appreciate about Susan's work is that she introduces us to Soul Alignment, which may seem to be 'up in the clouds' initially. In fact, she discusses aspects of being in alignment with ourselves so that we can work on a specific aspect of alignment directly! It is practical and down-to-earth.
—*Melanie Blau McDonald*

After I bought your first book, I bought five more copies and gave them to friends. Can't wait to read this next book in your series!
—*Beth Morrissey, Kleiman International*

Wow, this book is exactly what every single woman needs!!!! I keep writing down parts I loved and realized I had been writing a lot down! Every section is amazing! Every single section! *Feeling in control *Deciding what you want to feel *Deciding what will be fun. You KNOW I love the part about the importance of positivity!!! I am so proud of you, and your work is changing the mindset of so many!
—*Kelly Walk Hines, author of* RAK 'em Up, 200 Ideas to Spread Random Acts of Kindness, *author of* Memoirs of An Invisible Child, *author of* Hope in The Darkness

QUOTES BY OTHERS WHO HAVE DROPPED BY MY WEBSITE:

- Life-changing stuff for such a little book.

- I keep this little book in my purse to remind myself to breathe.

- Offering you clarity for confidence, comfort & soul connection.

- What an amazing book. I've read it twice and both times I've found new ways to look at my life. A must read for every woman looking to find peace and purpose in her life.

- I read Susan's 3 previous books and thoroughly enjoyed each of them. Her new publication, *Dear Future Self*, is an amazing addition to her work. It is relatable, easy to read, and allows space for self-reflections. Her phrases such as "see yourself for who you are" and "how to be Wonder Woman today and tomorrow" and "find your own authentic voice" allow for a reader to really do some deep introspective thinking. And it all leads to that happier and healthier self that she describes. Susan has done another wonderful job with her new book! 5 stars!

- Am I ready?" This is a question I had been asking myself. I just wasn't sure until I got through to the last chapter, 'Let Go.' And then, I knew I was ready!

ABOUT THE AUTHOR

Susan Axelrod, CCP, TIPC is the go-to Confidence Coach for Women. Specializing in working with executive women and matriarchs in mid-life who have spent decades doing for others and are now starting businesses or other personal endeavors in their 'second half.' Using co-creative & co-facilitative coaching methods, Susan helps clients uncover the inspired Soul within who is looking to live out life in a self-

fulfilling and purposeful way. Susan doesn't give answers or advice. She works with clients to dig into their core, to explore the girl she was and the woman she wants to be for the rest of her life, personally, professionally, spiritually, and physically. Using original Confident-Life™ Tools, Susan helps women find the Clarity and Confidence they seek to live out a *Best Life*. She works with women in transition who declare themselves 'READY!' ...ready to GROW, ready to LIVE now, in purposefulness and to create a meaningful legacy. Susan's contagious enthusiasm and deep listening skills sparks and motivates clients to get Confident and Thrive!

Looking for Motivational Speaking or Workshops? Susan's Confident-Life Workshops™ and speaking engagements are a hit every time! Available for work-teams, book clubs, friend groups, women CEO clubs, nonprofits or any place women gather. Using Tai Chi and Qigong as a basis to connect to Self, Susan weaves mindfulness and conscious awareness into everything she does.

Certifications:

- Certified Coach Practitioner, through The Coach Training Academy [accredited by the International Coaching Federation and Certified Coaches Alliance].
- Trauma Informed Professional Coach, certified through Lodestar.
- Qigong & Tai Chi Easy Level 1 Teacher, certified by the Institute of Integral Qigong & Tai Chi.

Other Books - Available on Amazon:

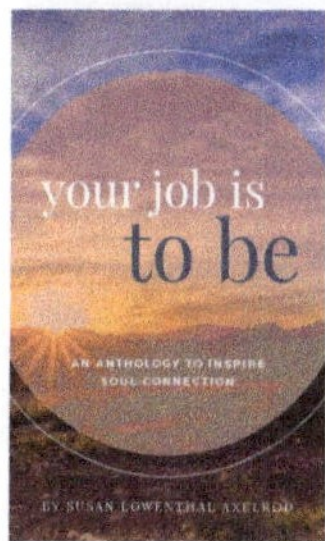

100% of the proceeds from these books support the global organization co-founded by the author, Jewish Girls Unite jewishgirlsunite.com

ARE YOU READY TO LIVE A MORE CONFIDENT-LIFE™?

Contact Susan now, you'll be glad you did. When you call, Susan responds. Everything is timely, 100% personal and 100% custom. Connect personally now for coaching, or to bring a Confident-Life Workshop™ or Motivational Speaker to your group. Learn about Susan and her work here: www.whatwillyourlegacybe.com.

CONTACT: susan@confident-life.com | 518-495-4573

I truly love to connect personally with my readers, I look forward to 'seeing you' anywhere!

- Look me up on FB or LinkedIn by my name, Susan Axelrod!

- Here's my FB biz page: 'What Will Your Legacy Be?'

- Here's my FB group: 'Discovering You Again for women in the second half of life'

- Here's my website: www.whatwillyourlegacybe.com

- My body of work lives on my YouTube Channel: The Confidence Zone with Coach Susan Axelrod. Type this into any search engine: youtube susan axelrod @ confidence zone

- Find my 5 books on Amazon, Author name-Susan Lowenthal Axelrod